T3-BGW-600

WITHDRAWN

INDELIBLE

WESLEYAN POETRY

INDELIBLE

Rachel Hadas

Wesleyan University Press
Middletown, Connecticut

Published by Wesleyan University Press,
Middletown, CT 06459
© 2001 by Rachel Hadas
All rights reserved
Printed in the Unites States of America

5   4   3   2   1

LIBRARY OF CONGRESS CATALOGING-IN-PUBLICATION DATA
Hadas, Rachel.
Indelible / Rachel Hadas.
p.   cm.
ISBN 0-8195-6439-7 (cloth : alk. paper) —
ISBN 0-8195-6440-0 (pbk. :alk. paper)
I. Title.
PS3558.A3116 I5   2001
811'.54—dc21   2001002136

CONTENTS

II

III

ACKNOWLEDGMENTS

The following poems have previously appeared, under different titles where indicated:

"Props," *Shenandoah*. "Four Short Stories," *Poetry*. "The Crust House," "Samian Morning, 1971," "Mourning's Dichotomy," "The Web" (previously "The Night Before Christmas"), "Motherless Fall," *New England Review*. "Pomegranate Variations," *Kenyon Review*; also *The Best American Poetry 1998* (Scribners), edited by John Hollander. "The Caravan," "The Banquet," "Humble Herb Is Rival to Prozac," "The Week After Easter," "Bedtime Stories," and "Recycling," *TriQuarterly Review*. "Around Lake Erie and Across the Hudson," *Literary Cavalcade*, also appeared in *Night Errands: How Poets Use Dreams* (University of Pittsburgh Press, 1999). "Helen Variations," "Rough Winds Do Shake," "The Genre Clerk," "Change Is the Stranger," *Arion*. "Fathers and Daughters, Mothers and Sons," "The Crust House," *Yale Review*. "Skirts," *Harvard Review*. "The Costume Chest," *Southwest Review*. "My Mother's Closet," *The Journal*. "The Light Bulb," "The Seamy Side," *Literary Imagination*. "The Letter," "Love and War," *Threepenny Review*. "Mud Season," *American Scholar*. "Homage to Winslow Homer," *Five Points*. "Thick and Thin," *Poetry Oxford*. "Déjà Vu," *Kenyon Review*. "Dream Houses," *Metropolitan Review*.

I

Thick and Thin

Time thickens.
Sticky, taffy-brown,
the malleable gunk of family
memories, resemblances, resentments,
anecdotes thumped and punched
by a succession of urgent hands
hardens and cools, but early lumps remain,
fingerprints, palmprints, even marks of teeth.
You spend a lifetime trying to smooth these out.

Time thins.
To the original mix nothing is added
but a steady trickle wrung from years,
a faintly salty broth, not tears, not sweat.
The solution weakens until only
a feeble fingerprint of this first scent
trembles half-imagined on the air.
That earliest essence—what was it again?
You spend a lifetime trying to get it back.

Samian Morning, 1971

The gypsy loomed in the open door of morning,
bulky, unsmiling, her head wrapped in a scarf.
Her hand was out. She wanted something from me.

I don't remember whether I faced her fully.
Had I looked her straight in the eye and then beyond her,
I would have seen the Aegean like a frame.
If I had looked far enough over her right shoulder,
I would have seen Patmos lifting in a strip of light
from the horizon's lip. Over her left
shoulder I could have craned and seen Ionia.
But both these radiant regions were blocked off
not only by the figure in the doorway.

Where had she come from? Behind the house was a field.
Beyond this square green field—it was a wheatfield—
were a bent fig tree and a low stone wall
and a whitewashed hut like a gatehouse. Behind the wall
a road wound north away from the coast to the village.
She could have just walked up Poseidon Street
to ours, the last house in the row. But I think
she came around from the side, the back, the North.
I used to think the wind blew straight from Russia.
Turkey was left, the East,
and right and West was the great granite mountain.

My stinginess and resentment balanced by shame,
I gave the gypsy something I remember
probably only because she scowled and reproached me.
Whether she came back a second time
to try again, another woman with her,
is wavering conjecture. But I see all right
the thing I gave her: bright yellow, cashmere,

still with its Saks Fifth Avenue label,
a sweater someone had given me, no doubt,
for the same reason I tried to palm it off
on the gypsy, who rejected it with scorn.
The sweater was marred. A stain like a port wine birthmark
splotched the front. Who would wear such a thing?
Not I. Not she. I recall the botched transaction
but have to supply the shining of the sea,
brilliant backdrop to the piebald life
I must have turned back to after the gypsy, grumbling,
took herself away from the open door,
though I do not know if I turned to it with relief.

Ghost Jam

Even if August spread out endlessly,
not all the blackberries
would ripen in one day. But equally,
to pick them piecemeal, one by one by one,
as each in turn
goes glitteringly black upon its own
inscrutable timetable can't be done.

I would be trapped in thorn and tapestry,
the leaves and mosses tarnishing each day;
step by step, finger by reaching finger
at first upon the border,
then deeper in the cool gulf of September,
each noontime clarity
more salient with its narrow blade of gold,
first only early mornings, then late mornings cold
and misty, so the ripest berries might
shine against wisps of white,
like black beacons, if black can give light.

And having filled
hours and containers with the cool
piles of glowing fruit,
I'd take it home and mash,
boil, stir, sweeten, strain
the hot dark stuff, its stinging purple stain
with sterilized jars (ready
to be filled with jam
then topped with paraffin),
their mouths agape
to take and taste and store and save the time,
the August, then September day, the hill
sealed in hot glassware set to slowly cool.

Would. Not *will.*
The blackberries this summer are behind
what I remember from a year ago.
Now when I venture to the prickly hill
I cannot lose myself or fill my pail.
For each long berry gleaming ebony
there are a dozen green or greenish red
or reddish black, all clinging tightly still.
And if the picker tugs impatiently,
the seeds feel woody, sour, dry,
no crushing in the mouth,
purpling of fingers, black perfume of fall.

But even if they ripened all at once
and early, and I had
a hundred hands and hours to spare, I know
that I would hear a low
call from behind the hill:
not loud but palpable, not shrill
but irresistible,
without whose urgent summons no
berries could muster this seductive glow;
without whose pull, strong and invisible,
from somewhere behind
the cold and golden, wet and tangled hill
I'd never lose myself in search of fruit.

Without the waiting world—
I do not see it yet, do not evoke,
only acknowledge it-
how could the berries keep
the mystery of their promise, sweet and black?
Once again this year I won't find out.
I hear the call
and I am going back.

Déjà Vu

A flap in time, a hinge in space, a secret drawer, a panel,
an unexpectedly discovered island in the river,
an instant confidence that is immediately forgotten
until, unless some utter stranger comes upon it later,
years later, less by rumor, instinct, chance, blind luck, or vision,
than memory. These discoveries are the future recollected,
a bump of time scooped from hereafter and transferred to now,
stolid duration's understudy, flashback of the future.

No wonder children (have I read this, heard, remembered,
    dreamed it?)
experience these interludes, these hidden flaps more strongly,
more urgently, as more uncanny, ghostly, and amazing
than those of us bowed down so blindly by the weight of days,
beyond astonishment, made numb by dint of repetition.
Children, with more they must experience, less they can
    remember,
itch to accumulate, take hold of even what is not
exactly now, precisely then, but somehow in between—
ghostly, prophetic, a quotidian-gilding vision
wrung from the flux, the might have been, the maybe, the
    abandoned,
the *oh I wish I hope I dream*, arcs of transcendent longing,
familiarity with lives unlived and yet available,
the haze not yet completely clear, all structures wreathed in mist
less blinding than what daily life is dully swaddled in,
each castle, tower, and labyrinth particular and gleaming,
each episode, each conversation burnished, fiercely clear.

The Last Time

In memory of William Matthews

Some people ambush you
and stop you in your tracks while at their pleasure
they tell you their endless story.
Others stamp right past you and ignore
your presence inches from their frozen face.
And others glide, they slope
around a corner, wry, amused, alert.

When I was last in Bill's vicinity,
we happened to be standing side by side
studying complex little mechanisms
(apple corer; tea ball; garlic press)
at Lechter's Housewares, where, for me, the old
Moon Palace's scar had yet to heal.
Still, there we were, intent in the same aisle,
absorbed as museum goers
halted before a single masterpiece.
We talked, predictably,
of flavors, kitchens, stores, the neighborhood,
and parted with a pair
of casual waves, vague but reciprocal.

And that was the last time.
But in what sense the last?
Not the last time the worn
Confederate soldier face,
the drooping mustache and distinctive limp
rose in my mind's eye. On the contrary.
So in what sense the last?
His passage left a ripple in the light.

The Caravan

in memory of Dulcie Holden Maynard

A blank dreams do their best to fill,
or smashing like a fist,
her lack maneuvers nightly
to make itself more space.

As if room for grieving
were only found between
the cracks of our continuing
campaign to love our own!

The urge in the grip of mourning,
the wish in the teeth of loss
is to retreat, fold inward,
and shrinkingly embrace

our dear ones, cherish all the more
our version of the life
lost by just the person
occasioning this grief.

Dulcie, so abruptly
erased from summer's map,
whom I remember bending
to children on her lap,

moves on now—we all do—
in the great caravan
composed of both the newly dead
and what still seems our own.

Painfully and slowly,
the pull is nonetheless
away from what we thought we knew
and loved to someplace else.

Mourning's Dichotomy

One task of mourning's to incorporate
fragments. Another says

keep faith with fragmentation.
Speech is pain and silence is defeat.

Words need to weave a filament between
opposing camps, yet silence must fit in.

While you were alive,
presence sometimes wore the guise of absence.

Now in the mirror world of afterwards.
absence resembles presence.

Around Lake Erie and Across the Hudson

in memory of Charles Barber

A rotten week, affections
grating against the grain.
I wake up, eyes beclouded
by the gift of dream.

First an anxious journey,
directions barely heard,
lockers, crowds, and tunnels,
the destination blurred . . .

but then, ah! calm perspective.
As if I were awake,
we three are slowly driving
around and round the lake.

You at the wheel, your sister
in front along with me.
Blue water, little whitecaps.
Brilliant October day.

You have a brand new haircut.
Your sweater's white and red.
Such vivid preparations—
as if life lay ahead.

Deliberately driving,
you cannot turn to me.
But conversation ripples
among us easily,

sister, friend, and brother
catching up: what's new?
And underneath the chitchat lie
two things we three know.

One, that we are joyful,
and two, this isn't real
miraculously coexist:
a miracle that still

tinges both past and future
with possibility,
although this outing never was
and will not ever be.

The shining lake; our chatter—
I carry them to work.
On New Jersey Transit
west out of New York

the rising sun behind the train
gilds pylons, bridge, gas tanks.
A purple cloud. A single gull.
I find I'm giving thanks.

The Glass of Milk

in memory of Paul Douglas

Not having seen him in a year or so,
I glimpsed him Sunday from across the street.
Perhaps I recognized him by his height;
his back was to me. Yet I thought "Oh no."
From a block away it was quite plain
the contours of his face were different: bone
newly sharpened, jutting at the cheek,
a smaller head atop a thin new neck.
And then he turned the corner and was gone.

I knew him only through the mutual friend,
well versed in what such gauntnesses portend,
who noted "the emergence of the bones
thoughtfully, when knowledge meets sadness
and it's just too late in the afternoon."
That friend is gone. But Paul I saw again
yesterday at the diner. Breakfast time—
a glass of milk gleamed. Not late afternoon.
Nevertheless for Paul the morning's done.

Mud Season

Alone in a white room,
and then to venture out.
Late winter. Watery glow
of melt and shining thaw
a second source of light.
Days lengthening. Me too.
Do not say young or old.
Do not say early, late.
Say that the ice is thin,
say that winter's cold
is giving way to spring,
so you can hear the voice
of reawakened water.
The month is winding down
and strips of snow are shining
underneath the moon,
except there is no snow.
The winter sheen is gone.
Beasts sleeping, curved brown backs:
the little hills are bare.
Pools give back the sky
and sky fills our boot tracks
so that we walk on air.

The Week After Easter: Heaven's Gate

Saturday. Suburban funeral.
Emerging into skimpy April sun,
"Of course what all this means is vertical,"
said my companion.
She sketched a swift diagonal
from heaven to hell—

gesture that left it up to me to trace
the arc in my imagination.
Golden forsythia haloed half the place,
but close up something dark was in slow motion:
a receiving line, inching along.
All this was horizontal. She was wrong.

Lift up your heart, the funeral mass advised.
My heart slid sideways as I eyed each face—
so many terrestrial creatures poised
at a mortal crossroads. East or west—
which way were we to head,
buttonholed by the living and the dead?

One bee last Sunday, drunk with its success,
negotiated blossoms in the park
where I was stretched out motionless
in blazing sun; who woke up in the dark
Monday morning to tattoos of hail,
magnolia blossoms battered in the gale.

Dramatic weather? Just a pale reflection
of Holy Week's impassioned allegory.
Hot on the heels of the Crucifixion,
the Resurrection salvages the story
and rescues history. Last yields to first,
the best redeemed—enabled—by the worst.

Silvery lilies, trumpet-tongued, proclaim
their clanging gospel to the air.
Exactly at this crux of space and time
believers throng toward a single stair,
a narrow window opening—a gate—
ladder to heaven. *Quick! Do not be late!*—

and vanish. We who opt to stay below
survive and flail,
coping with spring's successions: flowers/snow;
sunbath on Easter Sunday/ Monday, hail;
the agitated season's swoop and veer.
Tuesday noon, eyes narrowed from the glare

of sun on ice, I venture out in search
of solace? celebration?
Both, it seems; the florist's, atheists' church,
being my destination.
The warmth, the fragrant moisture . . . I breathe deep,
tugged by anxiety and stroked by hope.

People I love keep falling from the scene.
Their histories melt away like winter ice
in synch with leaves routinely turning green:
changes that must be faced. But both at once?
Arms full of flowers, I linger in the sweet
air inside, then move toward the street.

Dream Houses

The Dead Poet

Given a dream house, I know how I feel.
A year and more of honoring the dead
and a partition opens to reveal
two rooms where I had thought was only one.
Yet neither had a desk or chair or bed.
How, if he lived here, did he sleep or write?
In this authorial mausoleum
no worktable exists, no day, no night.
Less mausoleum, though, than cenotaph:
what pilgrims tramp through is a neutered place,
bare of his presence (that cocked head, that laugh)
and barer still of why they came to see
the residue of years in such a space,
empty of what he left us: poetry.

The Porch

Invited back in dreams, belatedly
I reconfigure how it must have been.
Of course in real life the house, being free
of porches, had a terraced roof instead,
like any venerable Athenian
edifice. Yet we sat on the front
porch—rickety, and various junk was spread
(clothes; motors) like a farmhouse in Vermont.
But on a second visit I was taken
indoors and through the dark interior
to the back porch. I hadn't been mistaken:
this was the privilege, the love, the joy,
this sitting softly talking till no more
light warmed any corner of the sky.

The Old Apartment

Given a dream house, once again I ride
north with incredible deliberation
up past 116th and Riverside.
Two fellow passengers talk to me in tandem
about their country and their destination.
Behind her face I peer, over his shoulder;
look out the window seemingly at random.
Greyness is growing, and it's getting colder.
Our glacial pace, though, clearly lets me see
the awning and the number and the stair.
Earl, the old doorman, would admonish me:
"Don't fall down, now!" as I went in and out.
Now people I don't know are living there,
their windows shining. We inch out of sight.

The Banquet

In both dreams about my father he is alive again, but in a public place: first in an auditorium after the lecture in a clump of people and then at a banquet where I'm an anonymous guest if I'm a guest at all.

My presence is either an embarrassment or else transparent.

In the first dream, although he acknowledged me I was one of a group surrounding him, so I had to wait in turn to congratulate him for the brilliant lecture.

But he was also me—talking to strangers, admired, greeted, distant.

In today's dawn dream he was at an official university banquet trying to persuade the carefully chosen administrators there of something. He was not the master of ceremonies, he was one more honored guest, but also somehow responsible for everything.

He got drunk with attention and began to be indiscreet, too emphatic, it was reported to me later.

Feta cheese crumbled visibly in his open mouth like a stigma of greed, but it was in the mouths of others as well. Still, things were becoming desperate.

And then offstage he was removed from the scene.

Offstage? As from a messenger in Greek tragedy I heard about it from my mother.

And I think it was I who broached the hard questions one after another: Is he in the hospital? Did he have a stroke? Can he speak?

and to each question the answer was the wrong one, the bad one, as I had known and she had known I would know it would be.

There was no chance, then, to say goodbye. He was removed invisibly, neither alive nor dead.

Not having been present, I lacked even the slightest sense of what the people with him there in the banquet hall had seen or exactly how when and why in detail it all happened.

Which is all minutely accurate, true of the actual death of my father as it was reported to me or rather as it never was reported in any detail at all.

So when people are thinking about how their second-hand Toyota truck with its 300,000 miles and its many journeys and various repairs is an emblem of their lives,

or—my own favorite—when they take stock of every stitch of clothing they're wearing, every piece of jewelry or scar, bruise, burn, cut, prosthetic device, or lovebite, exactly where and when and how they acquired it,

they might remember also to try to conjure in memory or recreate from eyewitness reports what the death (at which they were not present) of someone they loved might have been like.

But we have a built-in lack of curiosity, to say the least, about these matters; we are hardly permitted to get to the bedside, and we're not in a huge hurry even if we are permitted, and even if we are there then often we cannot bear to remember or perhaps are not even meant to remember precisely what it was we saw.

Thus when my mother died around noon the doctor called by two
to tell me but the machine was on and he left a message on the
machine for me to call him but did not—apparently doctors
are trained not to—leave word why I should call him,

and when I did call him at three or four his service could not get
through to him and the upshot was that I went to visit my
mother early that mild May evening and found her bed made
up, spick and span, empty in an empty room.

I had forgotten all this—it was almost five years ago—or rather
was evidently storing somewhere a perfect memory of it but I
had forgotten I remembered. Who wants to remember? And
who wants to forget?

But my dreams remembered, although in this dawn's dream my
mother appeared characteristically only in the ancillary guise
of messenger to tell me about the death of the protagonist as if
she were not herself worth remembering and mourning in the
dream as one who had also subsequently died.

The other disturbing detail was that at the beginning of the ban-
quet, which—have I already said this?—was some official
function sponsored by Columbia—

early in this dream feast the figure in the hot seat, as it were, was
not my father, it was my husband,

but he slipped away at some point midmeal as soundlessly as later
in the dream my father, who had replaced him, also did,

though not, I hope, I fear, for the same reason, mortal exhaustion
and terminal illness.

But the silent oiled automatic merciless quality of this disappear-
ance—these twin disappearances—made me lonely for him
on awakening and apprehensive,

love entering, as so often, late through a door marked Exit, the white world of the morning, the blank windows of day rich with the fading splendor of a dream about loss and silence,

leaving me as I woke with a clear image (but was it from after or before I opened my eyes?) of a shining white-painted ceiling and in the middle of it the nipple-like carved protrusion of an ornate floral arrangement,

the kind of ornament one might stare at while flat on one's back in bed or on a stretcher or on the floor

but also reminiscent of a wedding cake or any sort of centerpiece on a banquet table,

Miss Havisham's moldy wedding cake and the spiders silently rushing over it and over the ragged yellow-white lace tablecloth flashing through my mind at this point.

But not only was I unsure whether it was a dream vision or something I saw when I woke up or had seen at some time earlier, the day, the week, earlier in my life before;

I also had no way of knowing whether it was the last sight that had met my father's fading eyes at the very moment when he was felled at the white dream banquet

or for that matter whether in the dream this nipply thing had been seen by my husband as he was silently wheeled off the scene and replaced by an older man whom the same university had sheltered, Alma Mater, and worn out,

and I did not assist, French *assister,* to be present as at an event, but "assist" in English has a simpler, more active meaning,

I was not there to help them.

Humble Herb is Rival to Prozac

in memory of my mother

An item in *Science Tuesday* happens to catch my eye.
A woman in Germany
(it seems that she is only one of many)
having been drinking several cups a day
of Saint John's Wort brewed into tea
reports *The fear*
that everything good would disappear
has stopped.

Reading this, I seem to see
something shiny, peeling: elderly
Scotch tape, no longer strong enough to keep
the little sprigs in place, maintain the shape
of wild flowers picked and pressed
(though not pressed long enough to be quite flat—
even at five years old I probably
found time too slow:
"Those flowers must be all pressed flat by now!")
and taped into the pages of a smallish spiral notebook,
whose khaki cover
bulges with still bulky flower after flower.

Open the notebook. Turn the freighted page:
buttercup, clover, yarrow brown with age
or else pellucid—fragile either way.
Time has not only thoroughly discolored
the contents of this makeshift album, but
has begun the task of disassembling.
Delicate petals grow
amber-veined and clear;
tough little stalks now show

their pith; the tiny, no
longer yolk-gold tubelets
that form the daisy's eye
have gradually begun to come apart
and one by one escape
the sagging tape,
meander down the page
like stray eyelashes, like fluffs of lint.

Black-eyed Susan, Queen Anne's Lace,
found, picked, pressed, taped, and labeled;
aster, Devil's Paintbrush, everlasting,
St. John's Wort. Even then
I knew—I think I knew—this last-named flower
was rarer than the others. Knew it how?
Because she showed me the reliably
five-petaled pale gold blossom. Naturally,
knowing nothing, I had to be taught
every flower's name,
though probably I thought
Solomon's-seal, vetch, mullein, morning glory
were transparently my birthright,
as if all flowers hadn't come to me
through her who guided my unsteadily
printing pencil (1953);
whose disappearance (1992)
never made me fear
that everything good would disappear,
but teaches me, if anything, again
a lesson that each year I must relearn,
the renewable epiphany
of vanishing and then recovery.

The little notebook with my staggering
penciled captions labeling
every blessed thing,
picked and pressed and anchored to the page,

recording the first summer I remember;
her long full skirts, their cotton prints, the florals and batiks,
my clinging at knee level,
or her bending over
or leading me to the cowfield, where clover
and thyme attracted hordes of noisy bees,
showing me where this and that plant grew,
their names, and how to write them,
enlisting me in the whole enterprise
of writing, how to press a summer flat
between the pages of a heavy book—
what storage! what retrieval! what an arc
from something tiny as a daisy's eye
to something vast, too nebulous to hold—
the trail from recollection to invention
blazed and reblazed of necessity,
since memory can take us
only so far before it lets us down.

That bulgy little notebook
vanished years ago
and I no longer care
whether or not I find it.
Probably it's gathering
(even as it turns to) dust somewhere.
But laws of leaf and stem and petal hold:
what seems sheer desiccation
unlocks its stored, distilled
power into this brew,
this brimming mug whose steam
wreathes the lonely air:
Courage. Nothing good will disappear.

Motherless Fall

Which weep a loss forever new,
A void where heart on heart reposed;
And where warm hands have pressed and closed,
Silence, till I be silent too.

Tennyson, *In Memoriam*

Delicious in the afternoon
to wander, watch the sun go down,
and savor somber cadences,
sonorous, Tennysonian.

Autumn I enter like a ring
of darkness dreams prick with their pin,
speckling the black so that the mind
faintly glimmers before dawn.

Motherless fall: an empty field,
boundaries marked in ash or bone.
Late sun paints one apple-green
strip across the shady lawn.

Mourning changes: with each season
doors of successive stages open,
vistas into which I peer
seeking my mother's atmosphere,

wanting her presence or her voice
to warm the silence of this place,
to spin the thread of talk again.
Dead leaves rattle in the wind.

Merely by listening, mothers can
(judging from you) transform a pain
from adolescent stress and storm
into something tame, benign.

Nothing a child does feels quite real
till the cry "Mommy! Look at me!
Look, Ma, no hands! My symphony!
My sonnet!" stimulates a smile.

Who will now listen if not you?
You taught me language. What to say
without you here to answer me?
Will words dry up and blow away,

yellowing letters folded tight,
dead leaves crunching underfoot,
wavering phrases, faded ink,
so many stories doomed to rot?

Your face is lost, a lamp is out,
I can't make sense of what I see.
To read a presence, find a voice
takes conjurings of memory,

but all I know is Janus-faced,
is stubborn silence—also speech.
You are within and out of reach.
You can and cannot be embraced.

You are the sudden shower of rain
softening paths to muddy brown.
You are the single shaft of sun
illuminating afternoon

in the gazebo—cadences
lulling, comfortable, sad
that give me courage to explore
the barer landscape up ahead.

The Lost House

The lost house from the outside looking in:
family absent, but a panting dog
woofs up to welcome a wet woman, naked,
wrapped in a towel, who has just emerged
to lean on the locked door, look in the window.
Relative, tenant, visitor, or phantom,
who is she? Since the door is opened only
partially and reluctantly
by guilty lovers, no one ever sees
the whole place from inside or all at once—
or for that matter from the outside either,
so thick are the surrounding trees. Meanwhile
across the strait bright banks are visible,
farmland or hillside or another island.
Each stump and bush, each cultivated strip
is lit with tragic clarity no one
lost paradise could muster. Farm or coast,
cottage, island, all the bygone summers
have to work together to achieve
so preternaturally brilliant
an icon of the places I am losing,
have lost, will lose. Houses, chairs and windows,
curtains, books, the silver of the sea
southwest of Samos, or maybe the Atlantic—
these are sites at which I find myself
peering like a trespasser, a tourist.
Years I impinge on naked from outside
or try to enter, frantic,
wet, wordless, seeking shelter
as if I were entitled to go in.

In the Grove

Forster says in *Aspects of the Novel*
that fictional characters come in flat and round.
Let us apply this binary division
also to the living and the dead.

It may come as a surprise to learn
the living are the flat ones.
You might expect the dead
to shrink to two dimensions,

but no, they thicken, put on bulk and plumpness
until they seem more solid than the skinny
shapes of the living as we scurry past
always on our way to someplace else.

I mourn my dead when I remember them.
The round slim trunks from flat as cut-outs grow
full enough to lean against, to touch,
to walk through. I can slip

in among them or I can stand still,
thinking, breathing, maybe weeping, till
they come to me (occasionally they will).
I conjure them and then when they surround me

I pause in their pale grove
though always on my way to someplace else.
As is well known, the living are en route.
To where? We do not ask. We know the answer.

Why is it so hard to understand?
The living are flat. The dead
are round but out of reach.
Cry out to them; they are seldom near

or even if they hear they do not answer.
Next get this through your head:
the dead are flat. They stand
impassively in rows like dominoes

until they lean and one by one they fall.
Therefore it follows, fool,
that it is the living who are round,
the living who take up far too much room,

jostle and crowd. At whom
am I angry if not at the living?
When I remember them, as I have said,
I mourn my dead—

the ripple family, the hallowed ghosts
dappled and camouflaged in greenish shade.
My dead . . . We never seem to say *my living*.
We say *my loved ones*

and our mortality seeps through the phrase.
Loved ones: those we plan to leave behind
when we join the dead in their rustling grove,
yellow to green. The trees are out of time,

not like the living, who keep whizzing past
from here to there, exhaustingly en route
to where if not
this slope of trees I enter with a thought?

The Letter

New Year's evening, 1999.
Home from an unexciting open house
and not quite up to making resolutions,
instead of looking forward she looks back:
opens a desk drawer and rediscovers
what she all along had known was there
but had put the knowledge in the back of her mind.
It's time to pull the folder forward now,
and open it, turn over all the contents:
letters, postcards, the program
of the memorial service. One long letter
(the only long one, and the only typed one)
she reads again. Six pages single-spaced
take a while. And reading it she weeps.

Why? Wait. Rereading
anything worth reading in the first place
or even anything that seemed worth reading,
we take up a new text. (*Our Mutual Friend*,
a complicated brew of class and money
when I first read it thirty-odd years ago,
now strikes me as a contrapuntal cry
for what is out of reach—wealth, yes, and love,
and simply knowing how to read, as if
knowing how to read were ever simple.)
So this letter, dated June 4, 1990,
has changed. When it originally arrived,
it flew straight from her hands into her heart,
all but bypassing brain in its impatience
or her impatience. Now that there's no hurry,
she pauses, tries for the first time to picture
the circumstances under which he wrote it.

Characters in epistolary novels
spend more time writing about their lives than living them.
Compare The Way We Live Now, fax and e-mail,
cell phone and beeper (none of which was common
in 1990). Or do not compare.
It is a commonplace that what these time-
saving devices save us isn't time.
Imagine Darcy's or Frank Churchill's writer's cramp
after their long mornings at their desks
setting down with a candor and a patience
now inconceivable their twists and turns
of mind and heart, decisions and regrets
and new decisions. Though these gentlemen
had only as it were one hand apiece
in the epistolary world, they still
excused themselves from other obligations
and spent the morning writing, writing, writing.
To whom? Darcy to Elizabeth,
Frank Churchill to his father, yes of course.
Also to us.

The writer of the letter in her hand
had seen himself in something like this vein.
His letter to her had started as an impulse
that would allow a decorous retreat:
the guest, unwell
(a euphemism that the genre calls for),
retires after breakfast, after lunch
to an upstairs bedroom with an ocean view,
borrows a rusty manual typewriter
from his hostess, and begins a letter.
Did he make the visit in order to write the letter?
The letter was an elegant solution
to the problem of inhabiting two places
and neither place at once. Everyone gained
and no one lost. The epistolary genre
was a blueprint, script for solitude,

a chance to go upstairs and nurse his nausea,
hook up his catheter, address himself—
himself, another person, both at once.
It mattered then, it doesn't matter now.

When the letter reached her in the city,
the apartment was being painted. It was June
and hot. The cool blue-green of sea and headland
seen from his bedroom window and described
opened a casement in her; the word *love*
let in the sun. And reading his account,
rereading, rather, what she'd gulped down whole,
details she knew interlaced with names
of people she had never met or heard of,
hospitalizations, drugs, clam chowder, weather,
Maupassant tales, the color of the sea,
a dream of an old love, birds at the feeder,
a visit back when Granny was alive,
his disappointed hopes of being a writer,
there's nothing I want to do anymore,
she wept.

Reading it then and now, she wept and weeps
for what had been and was lost;
for the promise of what might have been
and never was; for what had never been
remotely promised but was nonetheless
so scrupulously preserved that she could hear
the quavering alto of his voice. Because
all he had hoped for had slipped from his grasp.
Because two years after he wrote the letter
he was blind, disoriented, helpless.
Because holding the letter she could feel him
crackling in the page between her fingers.
The recognition coupled with the strangeness,
the gift of confidence, of reminiscence
even of a life not shared; the glow of doomed

affection steeped each word
in sweetness. Doomed: he was mortally ill.
Affection: part of the letter's task was tracing
the path by which he had arrived at it.

And yet this time around
she's struck by the curious mix in the letter's tone
of confidence and anonymity.
It is a confession in a way,
but one that might be made to anybody—
message in a bottle tossed out to sea,
intimate tale told to a stranger in a train.
It's not surprising if she's now that stranger.
The reader even of a fresh love letter
has to supply the voice; behind the voice,
trembling, the texture of the tone.
This thought would have been heresy the day
the letter first arrived, its wings still wet,
its signals still a mirror to her heart;
now it seems second nature.
Letters do eventually change their spots,
emerging damp, translucent, and transformed,
as poems or as social history,
far from the tappings of a feverish house guest
one late spring evening somewhere near Cape Cod.
Time takes away the fever, the distraction,
takes away the dying house guest too,
ruthlessly, slowly, swiftly, in whatever order.
Affection, framed differently, is left.
Affection. Change. Patience. Desperation.
With what patient desperation
he wrote the letter; with what desperate patience
it waited in her drawer
1990 to 1999.

Painters were scraping the walls and spreading drop cloths.
She put away the letter in a drawer,
first having kissed it. Only later on
did it occur to her, if it ever did,
that despite our bland entitlement,
our solemn, greedy sense of what we're owed,
affection, however green with tears,
can't count on colonizing the future,
cannot always even face tomorrow,
but—striped in sun, blurred with salt water—throbs
even when facing back, away from the ever after.

II

Helen Variations

Ah non sol quelle che io canto o scrivo
Favole son, ma quanto temo o spero.
Tutto e menzogna, e delirando io vivo.

—Metastasio

There was a myth before the myth began,
Venerable and articulate and complete.

—Wallace Stevens

Three Heroines

Features worn harsh and flat,
whole body a clenched fist,
she offered her own breast
to the marauders—*Kill me, spare my son*
(or daughter; there were many, then were none).
Doomed bargain—who would savor such stale flesh?
The triumph in surviving everyone
was bitter, and her eyes as dry as salt,
her wrung-out belly hard as adamant.
One version calls her bitch, the barking one.

Given the choice, which one do I become?

The sister and the daughter,
the virgin sacrifice,
duped bride lured from her place
and dragged bound to the altar,
then, in one version, snatched away from danger
into a wilderness,
ambiguous haven from the land of lies,

into reunion with a brother,
rescue, revenge—but for the deadly snare
there had to be a late-exacted price.

Given the choice, which one do I become?

My bonny lies over the ocean . . .
Lightly she up and left.
The harbor boiled with ships,
but she was far away,
shrouded in mist, a ghost,
at once condemned, unrecognized, and lost
(waiting, according to one version, in
the patient amber of Egyptian sun)
and found. What if she was no longer young?
They had a place to sail to; they went home.

Given the choice, which one do I become?

Good Omens

All is auspicious, even
"Euripides's cave in Salamis
identified" (CNN).
Was Helen dark or fair?
Godlike, the director has the power
to choose even the color of her hair.
The costume designer ponders cruisewear.
And do my rhymes embarrass?
And what about the god from the machine?
It all will be embodied once again,
flickering and vivid as a dream,
magically hijacked and brought here.

Setting the Scene

An azure sea. A stretch of sand.
Pull of the voyage and return.
Stage set: a palace. Rather no,
make that a massive portico
and add a tomb where history
is laid to rest? To ossify.

Dramatis Personae

As at all reunions, one catches up on news.
And had you heard your mother hanged herself?
And has our daughter found a husband yet?

A hungry beggar wrapped in shreds of sail
humbles himself huffily at the gate
guarded by a leather-lunged concierge.

A stubborn woman huddles at a tomb.
And now a blustering king comes forth, whose sister—
a solemn virgin who foretells the future—

wavers among the choices of the day.

The Backstory

Behind these people lies
not what is carved in stone
but an alternate version,
the war fought for a cloud,
an explanation good
as any, grim reality denied.
Not that the soldiers never really died,
but the *I wasn't there*

and so it never really
happened, never could have happened feeling.
And add to this her weird immunity
from time and trouble, tucked
here out of harm's way
in this outlandish land,
its spread of sand,
its line of azure sea.

The Alibi

Mythology provided costumes, masks, and hooks
to hang them on, performances, occasions.
Is this the way it's serviceable, then,
labeling, placing, pigeonholing, gilding?

Try leaving everything
exactly as it was
back in the proem before time began,
abstracting time, removing it to clean it,
buffing it to a high
shine; subtracting time
and peering into the resulting zero
as through a porthole, as into a ring.

Palinode or alibi, escape
or waking from the nightmare of the war?

I thought I saw so clearly where the plot was going.
I knew the lines and the lines were all familiar,

the genealogies, the family tree
studded with brass tacks of geography.

But when the beauty's whisked up and away
over the battlefield and out of sight,

what's left? An absence in a woman's shape.
A hole torn from the web and the web trembles

and the whole story threatens to unravel,
the version so implausibly spun out.

Happily Every After

So let me tell you how it really happened.
There was no death, to start with.
Oh, soldiers died, yes, in a distant war,
all for a doll, a ghost, a figurine,

the rumor went round later,
all for a form compacted out of cloud.
But not now, here. And not this skin
sunbathed by mortality and time.

And what had the gods done?
Run it by me again.
A statue shaped of cloud, a forgery,
icon and ghost at once, idolatry
to fool the prime seducer,
to fool by filling up: to satisfy.

Captured at the zenith of that beauty,
the dead remained unchanged,
but then so did the living.
And with the living, not the alabaster of illusion,
and with the living, not the glorious dead,
it is our lot to live and so to be
hostages to mutability.
Though how much, really, did the situation change?

Menelaus finally found his Helen
alive and still desirable, if older—
oh, just a little older,
but then so was he;
a practical, a downsized immortality.

Slyly, triumphantly they sailed away
as the Dioscuri stepped forth upon their twin
pedestals of cloud with the announcement
that yes, their egg-hatched radiant half-sister
would die indeed, but only
into eternal life.

Of all her riches—patience,
cleverness, longevity, and beauty—
this was the most miraculous by far,
the grace achieved, sustained
through cloud and carnage, war,
exile and isolation and pursuit.

She wrapped herself within
a person, her own person, as in skin,
a magic mantle woven of the past,
glinting with visions, versions, alterations,
her node of myth a luminous protection,
the silky solipsism of her story.

Pomegranate Variations

Then sucked their fruit globes fair or red:
Sweeter than honey from the rock.
Stronger than man-rejoicing wine,
Clearer than water flowed that juice;
She never tasted such before,
How should it cloy with length of use?
　　　　　　—Christina Rossetti, *Goblin Market*

and thanks to Eavan Boland's "Pomegranate"

I

Most know the name. But since so many claim
ignorance of its color, nature, shape,
how can I do less than bring one in?

Next week, therefore, one makes its way to class.
I peel off the chartreuse
price tag: plunge in the dull

knife I've brought with me in my bag—not plunge,
rather gouge, pry, saw
and finally penetrate beneath the rind.

Lo and behold, the inside
looks nothing like the outside.
As a door is closed

upon a child still rosy from the bath,
pale partitions separate
clusters of ruby seeds.

Juice stains the silly knife, the paper napkins,
and the palm print-clouded plastic platter
which I now hand to the student on my left

nearest the door. "Here," I tell him. "Take
this, touch, taste it." "Which part do I eat?"
he asks. I say, "The seed."

II

I brought the pomegranate in because
(why else?) we'd read a poem called "Pomegranate,"
whose speaker, first the girl Persephone,
later on as mother turns to Ceres.

"Love and blackmail are the gist of it.
Ceres and Persephone the names.
And the best thing about the legend is
I can enter it anywhere. And have."

I brought the poem in because the textbook
chapter on symbolism and allegory
demanded fleshing out, as a globed fruit
asks for sun and rain. An antidote

to dryness, these twin spheres of tart pink water
yielding their juices to each lonely tongue,
first the pomegranate in the poem,
then the pomegranate on the plate.

III

Weeks passed, and I kept pulling words from them.
Not that they didn't have words already,
but to bring forth and test them, to expose them...
Words they discovered in their mouths like tongues,
blunt words, raw words, words to stash, to hoard,
and finally to build on. Words aren't children:
use them three times, they're yours forever.
Ignore them: you're the poorer, they are not.
Abuse them: you sound silly, they survive.

"Behind shut doors we're safe,"
I said. "Now out with it."
And they began to speak
and set speech down and write.
First sweetness stuck their words
together. Week by week
this honey soured to curse:
fuck and *shit* and *cunt*.
Testing the air, the water?
Measuring one another?
Spite for the world they had inherited,
poverty of the word-hoard they could claim?

I listen, ruthless; prod each wavering
impulse to grab and hold onto a name.

Call it a fruit. Call it the body's language,
renascent itch that says I am alive.
Sour sharpness, rose and green, a light like sunset
before a storm. The usual fresh crop
of eyes and lips. The usual
appetite for fruit: some touched, some tasted.
The one who said "What do I eat?"
pretended to be poisoned when he tasted,
mimed a violent tumbling from his chair.

IV

The door is shut. We glance at one another.
"Send it around," I say. The hoary spell:
Swallow a seed, you cannot leave this place.
Phantom figures on the page take shape:
Sheila's father playing cards with the devil;

Steve's carpenter ecstatic in the middle of nowhere,
happy as Christ, Mike ventures, in the desert
(even if Steve spells the word "dessert");
Janice's mother under whose tutelage
even Apollo would crunch.

I am not exempt. I eat a seed.
In Ormos once a pomegranate tree
stood in a back garden by the sea
where there also grew a lemon tree,
beans, and prickly okra six feet tall.

Picking that okra one hot summer dawn,
I suddenly made out a chameleon
motionless on the stalk, a violent green.
Did I cry out? Drop my basket? Run?
I was twenty-one.

V

The fruit we pass around is recollection,
trapped in this leathery russet fringed sphere
(small enough to fold a fist around)
of what had never really been known:

information, memory, or rumor
floating till now unanchored as a breath
now named, grown dense, made able to be held—
and yet, as if it is too hot to hold,

or else too heavy, passed from hand to hand,
sweet-sour globules locked inside, sensations
in cells enough for all of us to share,
synecdoche and globed idea of autumn,

mortality's pink slip,
ticket to a certain season . . . Wait!
The hour is over. Tentatively someone
from outside tries the door.

VI

The dream began and ended
on green blade of hill
severing a sunlit bowl
my mission was to fill.

Laps; vessels; upturned faces.
"What do we do with our hands,"
asked Homo Habilis as they straightened up,
"if not to mark the paths our minds have made?"

Ache in the hand from writing.
The sweet solution thinning, thinning, thinning,
the savor going watery and null.
With time so short, why hold back anything?

Already they are pressing at the door.
Ache in the jaw from talking.
Not that desire or energy are gone,
but see, this plethora of red partitions,

doors, desks, decorums, panels, skins, shells, rinds,
walls that hold in the secret of the fruit
which at a magic word spills out its sap,
scarlet, intoxicating, onto white.

Change is the Stranger

frondere Philemona Baucis,
Baucida conspexit senior frondere Philemon.
—Ovid, *Metamorphoses, 8.714–15.*

Ovid's *Metamorphoses* in Penguin
crumbling and yellowed. Not an ideal version—
Golding Innes Humphries Slavitt Martin—
but then no one of them achieves perfection.

Changes. By what stealthy alteration
does our amiable pink-gold cat
suddenly chirp and tread with her back feet?
What flipped the switch that brought her into heat?

Change. In the workshop at gmhc
one of the poets put it beautifully:
Change is the stranger that carries us away.
Then he in turn was seized upon as prey.

What was the predator? We identify
it by its swooping from a clear blue sky.
"The black bird's Death," I heard my son exclaim
when he was taken to the Terry Gilliam

film*Baron Munchausen.* And Sam,
his playmate, a year younger, echoed him:
"That black bird's Death." The two of them
in nursery school already knew his name,

wise in the ways of transformation.
For surely Death must take the odd vacation,
slip out of black and into something less
conspicuous. Mercury, Ovid tells us,

when visiting Philemon and Baucis
chose not to wear his wings. This tale my son,
ten years after Baron and black bird
(does he retain the faintest trace of those

early warnings of metamorphosis?)
reads through slowly, looking up a word,
puzzling at idoms, pausing to stroke
the cat, who answers with a topaz look.

Voracious death can pounce, or equally
turn bland, polite, invisible next day,
nowhere in the vicinity, just gone.
Children grasp as well as anyone

this jack-in-the-box intermittency;
better than grown-ups, better far then me.
Ovid knew, that master of disguise,
seductions, threats, pursuits, panicky cries.

His tangled tales of love entwined with fear
are threaded on the story of desire,
though vengeance is another crucial strand
for Ovid's episodic pearls. Offend

gods at your peril, do you inderstand?
Or else prepare to turn to laurel tree
or heifer, spider, dolphin, in the sea.
Those who would hold to their humanity

should keep their heads down, never dare aspire
to fame, skill, beauty, or celestial power.
(Although this rule's too simple—Philemon
and Baucis turn to trees on their front lawn,

sharing arboreal immortality,
as a reward for hopsitality
and happy marriage and longevity.)
What we cannot do is refuse to change.

Freeze any incident on Ovid's string
into an emblem, solid sculpted thing
which can be clasped and framed, can be contained
within the modest confines of a mind—

cat in a basket, sunbeam on the sill.
Being mortal, we then break the spell.
Permanence isn't in our repertory.
Surely as children who prolong a story

with *Then what happened? and what happened then?*
we shrink away from any kind of end,
happy or otherwise. But we gradually
yield to the power on the periphery

which seems asleep but has one open eye.
The golden cat wakes up and yawns and sqeaks.
George in earphones listens to next week's
assignment for Music Humanities:

Ave Maria's celestial paradoxes
composed by Josquin: *pia humilitas,
sine viro fecunditas.*
Jonathan looks up a final word

in Ovid. Ten years after the black bird,
he's having to remember transformation,
and turns to me for help with the translation:
"Now the old woman and the good old man

see each other *frondere*. What does that mean?
It can't be right. A person's not a tree."
"That's how the gods reward them, don't you see?"
I say a little bit too eagerly,

always quick to give the game away.
"They turn into twin trees perpetually,
flourishing forever side by side"—
a preferable fate to having died,

though when I read of bark that, rising, hides
their faces from each other, I do brood
about just how grateful we should be
to gracious Jove and kindly Mercury.

Virtue's rewarders? Agents of the power
that will transform us all at the last hour,
step forward at the close, snatch us away,
utterly changed from what we used to be.

III

The Genre Clerk

Would you prefer to see a transformation
or a raw transcript? Lyric? Metafiction?

Are you after accuracy of background
or did you wish to focus on the frame?

Was the ensemble of paramount importance
or will you zero in on one detail?

Alumni bulletin, epiphany,
dream journal, film treatment, fable, myth,

ribbon of consciousness rolled and unreeling
across the floor and underneath a table

then to be disentangled
or left in all its aleatory loops . . .

Open a window to the glare of noon.
Let there be—nope. Pull down the shades; but first

fix the passers-by as they go about their business
in a burnished allegoric frieze.

That can be your centerpiece. And you—
looking at options, making up your mind,

leaning on the counter, indecisive—
are part of this unfolding story too.

Four Short Stories

One. In the opening speech of *Agamemnon*
the Watchman, fearing indiscretion, yields
the burden of exposure to the palace:
"This house itself, had it a voice, would speak."

Two. When describing almost any group,
encounter, reading, party, scene, my friend
habitually (parenthetically) says "Then
I turned to X and said,"

and by supplying what he said to X
doubly distances the incident,
himself both chorus to the scene evoked
and messenger of the chorus's response.

It's catching. Lately I have heard myself
interpolate my own accounts of life.
"And then," I keep on hearing myself say,
"I turned to So and So," etcetera.

Three. March sunlight stripes the corner table
of the cafe where a left-handed man
hunches over a notebook. From the aisle
I glance at the two phrases his curled hand

has incompletely shielded from such snooping:
I seem   I always seem to   What? and why?
Since he's already set the pattern down,
instinctively I wish to fill it out,

furnishing incidents and motivation,
plums in the endless pudding of narration.
And four. The concertgoer next to me
whose brooch I've just admired at intermission

accepts the compliment by promising
to spin a yarn in which her pin will figure:
it lacks a voice but oh, what it could tell!
She tells its story till the lights go down.

The Costume Chest

The costume chest is ransacked; an old play
is in rehearsal. For the new production,
freedom allows (or else necessity
enforces) variation, reinvention.
I'm taken by surprise at the audition,
not having known the heroine could be
somber or frivolous or dark or fair
or that a role could ever fall to me.
I thought that as translator of the play,
shielded in invisibility,
I'd be exempt from having to appear.
No one's exempt. I look around each day
and notice characters of every age,
both sexes, move without self-consciousness
as if their whole lives had been lived on stage,
in makeup, costume . . . Here's the sullen page
(really a slim girl in drab disguise);
the giddy redhead with the heart of gold;
cushiony mother, predatory man—
have they all learned their parts so quickly, then?

One swift twist of the kaleidoscope
and the whole production starts again.
A new script is dealt out to everyone,
or, in the new play, a different role.
Or someone new directs, or must revise
the recognition scene past recognition.
Where does the authority come from?
How to take courage, how to improvise?
And how to be one person through it all?
Yet since at bottom people stay the same,
how not to be one person? Two and one—
reverses flipping over like a coin.

Our lives are spent in gnawing at this bone.
We're thick-skinned creatures who absorb a fact
best if it's in the lines we have to act.
What others tell us we can hardly learn
unless we put that person's costume on,
garment of selfhood, memory, and pain.
Playing a part will show us who we were
once, or will be, or already are—
will teach us all we're able to take in
of how it feels to wear another's skin.

Props

The Queen steps forward, strews the open grave
with white rose petals. "Sweets to the sweet!"
Although the courtiers, mourners, family, priest
soon sweep away toward their next appointment
(for every man hath business and desires),
a few curved petals on the dusty stage
stay through the quick debriefing with Horatio,
through Osric's visit and the fencing match
still gleaming. Even when they lift the body
high, while the livid King and Queen are sprawled
half-in half-out of armchairs, some few white
remembrances remain to be discerned
by your sharp eyes. You said you hardly grasped
a word of what was said; nevertheless
this much you spied.

          As when Jocasta
lays offerings on the altar—*May it all
be well!*—which are still there
sending their threads of savory smoke aloft
when the great cry comes; when the messenger
bursts in to tell us she has hanged herself.

Homage to Winslow Homer

Wringing out her heavy woollen skirt,
a tall girl with one dripping flaxen pigtail
stands, head tilted to clear
the water from an ear.
Not too far beyond her on the beach,
six, seven, eight small boys—they form a troop—
splash, boast, shriek, leap, skip stones.
Beyond them, it's just possible to spy
clusters of little girls in twos and threes
sitting, heads together, on the sand.
Or else, still grouped, some stand,
stockings off and ankle-deep in water.
One holds a doll;
one points out to another
the pink and glossy inside of a shell.
The pale cool noon lighting a northern summer
glazes it all,
sails on the horizon, dancing water.

Wait. Since the girls are turned away, and small,
part of the background of this painting, how
can I be so sure what they are doing?
I have been there.
I know.

Recycling

If from ruined Tara's draperies
Scarlett O'Hara made herself a gown;
if at Bryn Mawr during the Depression
my mother's classmates used to sew their own

skirts out of curtains; and if the long rugs
Samian women used to weave for us
contained rag strips I'd cut out of my old
blue jeans or nightgown or flowered sun dress,

then I'm just carrying on a long tradition,
since everything I can reuse I will,
as long as it is paper: index cards,
jiffy bags, folders, bluebooks by the pile.

Any twice-used index card will tell
two stories, thanks to Janus, one per side.
Turned over, today's shopping list recites
the names of poems and just where I tried

to publish them in 1975;
Columbia admissions information
(my mother used to work for them part-time);
or bibliography for my dissertation.

Rough drafts of poems, essays, book reviews;
manuscripts sent by many a trusting friend;
contest entries, articles, exams—
of paper there will never be an end.

I give some to the super. Quite a lot
I keep as drawing paper for my son.
Some I dump into the recycling bin.
Some I cut up and put beside the phone.

Index cards, bookmarks, and matchbook covers—
any heavy stock—my father used to shred
to straw-sized markers for the text in use,
a practice I seem to have inherited,

recycling thus the habit of recycling,
approximating printed matter to
something like compost—an economy
by precept or example learned from you,

Daddy. Of course not every paper's sliced.
Jiffy bags are sent back whence they came,
into the world to someone else's desk.
My favorite recycling, though, stays home.

Flocks of manila folders drift my way,
shedding the contents of their former selves—
courses I've taught, my mother's tax returns—
but most of all from my friend Charlie's shelves.

His clipping files on writers he adored
no one could bring themselves to throw away.
His poetry collection came to me,
these folders tucked inside it like a stowaway.

I weeded through the clippings; earned the right
to toss each separate yellowing review,
but kept the folders, heavy, clean, and marked
in the loose clear printing that I knew

Sylvia Townsend Warner, Reynolds Price,
Williams and *Auden, Sarton* and *Vidal* . . .
Our tastes, not coinciding, overlapped
for far more folders than I can recall.

Here was recycling! Shorthand, slim, compact,
whole oeuvres signified by name alone,
each folder a synecdoche for worlds
my friend had loved to dwell in. He is gone

and incorporeal now, like literature.
Books too fat to fit in folders still
endure as reference, memory, and love,
recycled, feather-light, perennial.

Skirts

Deep-girdled, deep-bosomed, floating-gowned—
generic or Homeric terms for what
sways even today above the ground
somewhere between the ankle and the knee.
If I had to concoct an epithet
for women facing fifty, I'd say *vast—
skirted*—longish, full, and swinging free,
and gathered (not too tightly) at the waist,
whose well-worn cottons—calico, batik,
faded denim—furnish a good gauge
(s single downward glance, no need to speak)
less of chronology or build than how
we carry it, this soft, this post-maternal age
enfolding half our bodies, old and new.

My Mother's Closet

When we rummage through
the wardrobes of the dead,
are we not combining
reunion, disguise, and hiding place?
All these are the specialties of dreams.

Into—no, out of my mother's closet
I awoke from a dream of *Hamlet*.
I was cast as Hamlet, hero, prince—
no contradiction that I was a woman
and still alive. Had the tragedy
turned inside out into a comedy?
I'd gone away toward the end
and was trying to return in secret
as Hamlet does from shipboard in Act IV.
There had to be, then, one more act to come.
Nevertheless I'd managed to get home,
but whether in order to ransack her closet
for a disguise or lie low there awhile
or simply visit—all these motivations
were packed into a single narrow space.

The Queen dies at the end, which wasn't yet.
My mother's dead, although not in the dream.
Queen in the dreamplay. Loved me.
Anxious about me in the dangerous court,
anxious about my departure,
anxious about my clandestine return,
as mothers are, and helpless, too, to help me,
as mothers are. I woke up struggling,
my right, my writing hand, my whole right arm
clenched and bent painfully under the pillow.
Had I been taking ghost dictation?

Or into what improbable disguises
had I been attempting to insert
my alarmingly clumsy and recalcitrant body?
Cumbersome petticoats, tight pointed shoes,
layer upon layer of dresses. In the closet
were crammed not a queen's robes but an old lady's—
lumpy white cardigan, green-flowered dress—
hanging there empty, like my mother's clothes
when I and my sister opened her closet door
and hurriedly chose things for her to wear.
Helping her get dressed felt strange, belated.
Her closetful would soon, as we both knew,
be given away and kept at the same time,
relegated to the realm of dream.

Going through what one's mother no longer needs
to see what fits and simply to take stock
is what women growing older do.
And not just women, and not clothes alone.
"Into my grave I'll wear that Yes of theirs,"
wrote J. of his acquired Greek nod (our headshake).
Did my mother wear Yes to the grave?
Does Hamlet? How she loved the play. Will I?
The dream, not having reached Act V, won't say,
although the dream-script also writes the waking day.
Nights I go to my temporary grave
bathed in the retrospective tide of books
and in the prospective tide of dreams—
the tide of books goes out, the tide of dreams comes in—
grateful for having seen and read and seen
Hamlet over and over
even in the black box of my skull.
Courage! The lights go down
and each night's theater
flowers into color, motion, sound,
the clenched fist of the dreamer
vainly struggling to take it down.

The closet full of costumes
opened, but only to the sleeper's eye,
just as the dreamplay opened out and out
by folding inward, taking up no space.
Both play and closet
were bigger on the inside than the outside.
The closet was in the play
but the play was in the closet.
Think of Lucy fumbling among fur coats
in *The Lion, the Witch, and the Wardrobe*
who finds herself abruptly not in a musty wardrobe
in an abandoned room in the countryside in wartime
but in a frozen forest at night in a magic country.
Yet between the trees she can still just make out
the wardrobe's open door and through it daylight.
It was as I was fingering my mother's
unqueenly sweaters, shirtwaists, jerseys, pants
that the stage lights failed and I found myself
confronting daylight, my disguise half on,
home for a little, poised to leave again.

Sisters

Two women staring in a single mirror,
both hazel-eyed. Whose eyes are bluer? greener?
No way to tell. This overlap is why
we strained to disentangle, you and I.

It seems to me that I refused to like
things I thought you cared about. But what?
The only instances that come to mind
resemble Helen Schlegel (*Howards End)*

following where her elder sister led
"though with a more irresponsible tread."
Reading the novel at fourteen, I saw
these two could easily be me and you.

On Sunday mornings while our parents slept,
for years we played with paper dolls. Played? Kept
adding to the narrative we shared
about the dolls (shared also)—who, with flared

Fifties skirts and high heels were, of course,
coed dolls, whom we followed in due course
as one by one (you in pursuit of knowledge,
me panting in your wake) we went to college,

where doll play wasn't talked about. Instead
separate adventures in and out of bed
took over, drama trumping narrative.
No time to tell—there was too much to live.

Love and death got stirred into a mix
sampled, digested differently by each.
Books, then? You alphabetized the shelves; I couldn't,
or never thought of doing it. I didn't

major in English, partly since you had
and partly since I reckoned I could read
Dickens and Keats, Shakespeare and Eliot
on my own; Tibullus, Pindar not.

Just when our tastes in reading ramified
I'm not sure. By the time our father died
we had, no doubt, our individual
attitudes toward the books that lined a wall

we had faced, growing up, at every meal
(though as I try to reconstruct it, I
think I faced the books and you faced me,
or did I dream this?). Books furnished that room

and certainly still furnish yours and mine—
our space, our stanzas, how we work and play.
In our fifties the similarity
stays striking, even if you like true crime

and Larry McMurtry, while I incline to rhyme.
As undergraduates, you read Miller on
sex while I ploughed through the lexicon;
while you roamed jungles following Levi-Strauss,

my Greek class slowly snaked through *Oedipus*.
From this distance here is what I see:
we moved toward one end circuitously.
Each life does this; each pair of lives does too,

so there is nothing startlingly new
in our sororial spiral, far, then near,
repeated till we singly disappear.
And yet, as story told replaces act,

the symmetry's remarkable. The fact
of ordinary aging, gravity
tugging our flesh (we've both had surgery),
the slow transparent way we move through time,

or it through us, feel stately and sublime,
reassuring in their solemn rhythm.
Gems in one kaleidoscope, we pause,
patterned according to eternal laws.

A poem in words of one syllable
switches from verb to noun or back at will,
so actions keep eliding into states
of being, back to gestures that we make,

choices and motions, then again to pure
stasis, which we scan the mirror for,
seeking resemblances (what else is new?)
between the things we name and what we do.

Skewedly or shrewdly sizing up, we trace
in the mirror's uninflected face
change looking sideways at her sister change,
familiar features melting into strange.

We gaze at one another, and our gaze
twists like a living thing; our own surprise
surprises us. You take my hand, and I
hand you a copy, and you copy me.

We scan the copy, and our hazel glance
pools its skeptical intelligence,
two women looking in one crowded mirror,
similar and separate and together.

The Light Bulb

Yesterday Owen Barfield died at ninety-nine.
As my mother said of Rudy Vallee
when I read her his obituary
the day before she died,
I had no idea he was still alive.

The section of the myriad-sectioned Times
with Barfield's obit—now, where did I put it?
Under the cat's bowl? Underneath her box?
One or more of Owen Barfield's books
is surely on the shelf. He must have something

urgent to say to me. But where to look?
The world is full of clues
and to follow any one of them
you have to find it first (persistent ringing
of a cordless phone under a pile of junk)

and then—no, simultaneously—you have
to brush past endless other hanging webs—
their many beckonings, their drops of brightness—
focusing on a half-forgotten goal,
yet open to the world along the way.

Recently over lunch a friend unearthed
a light bulb in a story that my sister
wrote as a high school sophomore or junior:
algebra, humid afternoon with greenish
Ode to Dejection light. The heroine,

on her way home from Hunter High School, somehow
is handed, at a construction site, a light bulb,
accepts it, takes it home—a talisman.
My sister knew the Narnia stories well.
There always was about her, says our friend,

paying the bill and shrugging on her coat,
an inner light, only she never knew it.
Or else she has forgotten what she knew.
The time, the place, the visionary dreariness
of the Manhattan streets through which the story's

heroine roams both is and isn't so
deeply familiar to me (with that weird
inward domesticity of dreams)
that I had no way to measure whether
I was hearing the story of my sister's story

for the first time that day or had always known it
or had dreamed it and was only now
reminded of my dream. This much I knew:
I wasn't wholly lost in the labyrinth.
Part of me in broad daylight recognized

a smallish object, radiant and dingy
whether seen from a distance or up close.
It winked and twinkled, modest, uninsistent.
I sleepwalk to the shelf and take down Barfield's
Saving the Appearances: A Study in Allegory.

The obit notes that Barfield used to take
long walks with C.S. Lewis (the two friends
called themselves the "cretaceous perambulators")
and that Lewis dedicated *The Lion, the Witch, and the Wardrobe*
to Barfield's daughter Lucy.

Fathers and Daughters, Mothers and Sons

My father died in August. All that fall
the sight of happy father-daughter pairs
stabbed me. At the desk in Whitman Hall
I had to turn my head to hide the tears,
seeing a junior kiss her dad goodbye.
He'd taken her to dinner. Aquiline,
smiling, sallow, unmistakably
akin . . . And I: what father now was mine?
a voice demanded histrionically
inside my head. What likeness could I claim?
Only sorrow, and a secret shame.

And that was thirty years ago. The ache,
having moved inward, buried splinter-wise,
for decades, lately has begun to make
marked if sporadic reappearances
halfway to pleasure—more than halfway there.
As Aristotle says, mimesis is
why we turn to art, why we can bear
sorrow once captured in performances,
catharsis moistening the driest eyes.
Dilemmas shaped in skillful imitation
turn pain into a source of consolation.

Agee's "Knoxville Summer of 1915," set
by Barber, which I lately heard performed,
gave such a boundless, such a bittersweet
sense of the child's tranced safety—drowsy, charmed
by his triumphant luck at being here
now in the cicada-shrilling dark
with parents who would never disappear—

that recognition did its deadly work.
I groped for kleenex for the sudden tears
that signaled less self-pity for the past
than joy such ancient losses still weren't lost.

Yet art's mysterious power of transformation
has changed the focus, so that though the tone
of Agee's lyrical imagination
reanimated losses of my own,
I could no longer be the child ensconced
between its parents. Now I was a mother,
and the bereavement I had suffered once
changed as I wiped my eyes into another
of the life cycle's scattered pressure points,
always dormant till a sudden shock
of recognition makes us start awake.

I am a mother. And my son is where?
Away at camp. No, that's not what I mean.
Where is he in the heart's interior?
Or where do memory's labyrinthine
passages conceal the pivotal
moment when—let's not say that childhood passed,
but rather love began to flow uphill?
In Proust the longed-for kiss does come at last
to him who waits. I'm not so sure it will
once love's arrow changes its direction
and Mom's the one who waits for some affection.

I think back to an endless afternoon.
Humidity was high, ambition low.
School was out. We inched toward mid-June
with a piano recital still to go
and other chores, before our true vacations
out of the city. (When does life begin
feeling like a string of obligations?)

Sticky, groggy, listless, I gave in
and stretched out for a nap. My best vocation
having been always taking books to bed,
for what seemed hours and hours I dozed or read

a history of the Olympia Press,
sinking and bobbing in and out of slumber.
Southern, Nabokov, and Girodias . . .
And next to me my son, the latest number
of *Dungeon Master* or *Nintendo Power*
under his arm, lay down. So, parallel,
we partly napped and partly studied our
respective reading matter till night fell.
Tranquillity: an open-ended hour,
a humid hollow in a sleepy day,
an interlude we filled up silently.

The tempo quickened soon, as tempos will,
and life resumed a more demanding pace,
the fuss and flurry of departure, till
summer's separation carved a space
from which I found I suddenly could see,
remote and burnished through the double glaze
of time and distance with great clarity
a simple sight imprinted on my gaze:
not an epiphany, just a lanky boy.
Curled up reading, his long legs a Z,
he turns a page and sighs contentedly.

Leave him a little, reading on the bed.
Let time move forward as it always does,
his summer melting into seventh grade.
There's one more moment where I want to pause:
one chilly Friday morning in late fall.
He's home from school and feverish with flu.
A carpenter, here measuring the wall

for bookshelves, shakes his head: "Oh, man. Me too.
I've been sick all week. What can I do?
You got to work. But this is when I miss
my mother. Men need moms to care for us."

The carpenter went back to noting down
measurements. The boy dog-eared a page.
I drifted to the kitchen to put on
the kettle, in a cloud of youth and age.
The grief attached to us!—a leg, an arm,
habitual and almost effortless
until a chance remark sounds the alarm.
alerts us to the permanence of loss
so deeply rooted, so much part of us
a random rhythm, season, smile all may
transform the hollow to a memory.

Missing is one more form of loving—sad,
but not as sad as never having known
a mother who brought tea to us in bed.
Sneezing, the carpenter (he's my age) climbs down
his stepladder and starts to pack his things.
The cat sits on the bed to wash her face.
I bring a tray in. Life on silent wings
wafts us to a slightly different place,
a temporary level of repose,
a plateau where momentarily
love is something that we name and see.

The aura of the comforting and lost,
the halo we ascribe to what is gone
and not to be recovered! If the past
is the one place where feeling can be seen,
it still is not a place we can sit down,
put down our luggage, up our feet, and stay.
Its only mode is visions of what's been—

rare and fleeting, I was going to say.
And yet how often, as the years go by,
messages make their way somehow or other:
a friendly stranger thinking of his mother.

Rough Winds Do Shake

The usual dog-scrutinizing walk,
mother and son, up West End Avenue.
Admiring one dainty, silken creature,
I say incautiously "Isn't she sweet?
Look at that darling dog!"
                              You acquiesce
(or rather I assume you acquiesce;
usually our dog tastes coincide)
as far as the next stop light, silently.
Then: "Did you invent that word?"
                              "What word?"
"*Darling.* I've never heard
anyone say it, ever, except you."

"Of course I didn't invent it.
Remember Captain Darling
in the "Blackadder" we watched last night?"

Feeble response, I'm perfectly aware—
as if a name proved anything. I try
to call up other darlings, but my mind's
a blank—I'll check the OED at home.
No, not a blank. I hear my mother's voice:
Good night, darling. Or was it good bye?
Over the years, both; one and then the other.

How did this impassioned substantive
go adjectival, gooey, sentimental,
above all so maternal? There's the rub.
"Okay," I say. "I see that you think "darling"
is a finky word."
                              "Finky," you reply
in withering tones. "Don't use that word either."

My Father's O.S.S. File

News from inside: electrocardiogram
last week, and chest x-ray. From last night's dream:
at Riverside Drive and Seventy-second Street
a flood whose waters are "five thousand feet
deep." From a frontier of sanity:
the manic guy obsessed with poetry
stops sending letters, starts to telephone.
The thirteen year-old in his room alone
slams the door and then turns up his amp.
Peach and rose, spring sunset lights its lamp,
gilding the river's ribbon and the trees,
whereupon a designated Muse,
unconscious, radiant, strolls toward Broadway.

Not one but two young women yesterday
asked me to share the secret of my life:
the almost twenty years I've been a wife.
I may as well refer them to the file
that suddenly arrived in today's mail
if they want data. Secret? I don't know.
Who can retrace the paths that brought her to
the latest crossroads? But it seems we do
(this much I know) pass the next generation
coded heirlooms—patience, desperation,
fear and habit, boredom and desire.
Now I hear him playing his guitar.

Eye Level

My loss; your window. At the very moment
you looked at me, I happened to be looking
back over my shoulder.
But I turned in time
so there was just an instant eye to eye,
the passage at eye level, glancingly.
The day will come, and soon,
when you will pass me by.
When you are indubitably
taller than I am or will ever be,
who will I be then?
You who were looking in
at that very moment turned away—
not Orpheus and not Eurydice,
but the preoccupations of a day,
but the familiar gone invisible.
Just possibly you saw yourself in me
and seeing through that window looked away.

Last Afternoon in Athens

The call at the cluttered apartment
of the old friend who's still living;

the stroll past the shuttered house
of the other old friend who's dead;

both visits done, it's all downhill from here
(stairs for me and banisters for you)

from the mountain to the heart of town
where to kill time before the sun goes down

we drop in on an earthly paradise—
the National Garden. Here a crone

feeding hordes of cats shrieks *Go away!*
Leave them alone! They're hungry—let them eat!

Obediently we sink into a seat
from whose respectful distance we can watch

tigers, tabbies, tortoise shells, black, white,
tiny, lordly, dive and yawn

and stretch in striped sunlight.
We neither talk nor look away

from this teeming nursery. Dusty leaves,
the paths, the bench, the stones

look soiled and ancient, glazed with knowing sun.
Still speechless, we stand up in unison.

Love and War

7:45 on a bright May morning.
My son and I—our usual weekday routine—
leaving home together, pause. Without warning
we both have seen

an identical double apparition:
blond boy in shorts (Jon knows him from school) embraces
girl, standing stock-still, petrified with passion,
each of their faces

buried in the other's chest, or else gazing
vaguely outward, solemn and blank and blissful,
she on tiptoe, her two feet barely grazing
ground, since he is tall-

er. If one fell, both would go down together.
Living emblem, two halves of love's young rhyme,
splendidly heedless of passersby, schoolbus, weather.
There is no time

to look longer. Tearing my gaze away,
I trudge to the newsstand. There, before heading back,
in the morning's second swift glance I see
headlines in Greek.

Hellenic rendering of the Balkan crisis:
mercenaries, bombs, dire provocation.
What Nato gains/ what does Nato gain (the two phrases
sans punctuation

are identical). Also: Three American
Prisoners Released. *Aichmalotoi* rings a bell. How
far does it go back, that familiar noun?
To Homer or so?

If the noun is old, how much more the thing.
Home again, the stolidly Anglophone
Times tucked under my arm, I take magnifying
glass, lexicon,

learn Herodotus was the first to use
the term *Aichmalotos* (POW). As for the
provenance, the etymology of today's
embrace: it's me

and you—is, was all of us, now and then.
The youthful tense oblivion of a creature
struggling vainly to merge with another one
is part of nature

old when a poet pictured the apple so
tightly clinging to the bough, out of reach.
though the expression "prisoner of war" was no
doubt in the speech

she deployed. Love, war: Sappho weighed the two.
Some people say that *chariots, cavalry*
are the world's most glorious sight; but no.
At least for me

beauty's in whatever we love most. I,
loving Anactoria more than ranks
(eyes in her pale face stars in a cloudy sky)
of planes and tanks,

find her the most beautiful. She makes use
of war's panoply as a yardstick for ardor.
When I got back home, by the way, the bus
had passed our corner,

taking with it half of the double vision
tightly intertwined in the morning light
and my son away to an education
in God knows what.

Bedtime Stories

In Key West I visited D.J.
Naked, the old man smoked in bed all day.
And what was he to me?
I wept as I sat with him for an hour
chatting about the future and the past—
partly for him, but more
for someone he'd improbably survived.
Of course there was also the memory
of D's kindness thirty years before
in Athens, where he helped me find a job
and an apartment, even lent me sheets.
I sat with him, tears running down my face
for someone else. Oh, love is all displaced.

In various hospitals, in their apartments,
I visited four, five, six dying men.
And what were they to me?
Poetry students. And I to them?
Teacher, colleague, one more local friend—
the chitchat of the living. Even so,
conversation labored toward the end,
limping as unilateral dialogues do.
Talking to D.J. was like that too,
or yearly visits to my mother-in-law:
answering a question no one's asked
while a dumb monster presses its dull mass
against the window. Love is all displaced.

Dan, at Cabrini, talked and laughed and sang,
but that was several months before the end.
Diapered neatly, Tony lay at home
on the bottom bunk. I tried to tell him
about a play I'd seen. He tried to nod.

Or did he? Michael squeezed my hand. Or did he?
In Sloane-Kettering, James for the first time
sounded afraid. A bastion of pillows
propping Charlie up on my last visit
kept threatening to topple. As I was leaving,
his parents hurried in fresh from the airport.
I folded my grief small to give theirs space
as our paths crossed. Oh, love is all displaced.

His somber loneliness a smoky blaze,
an elderly heart surgeon falls for me.
He stares all through my talk on poetry,
asks me to Christmas cocktails at the Plaza.
How can I know—it's summer—I'll be busy then?
My middle age—my fragrant youth, for him—
is mesmerized months later, moth to flame,
by a man young enough to be my son—
teaches my son guitar, is twenty-four,
looks like a Quattrocento lutanist.
Romantic comedy? The prickly taste
of farce? Blind Cupid's arrow in each breast?
Whichever, love is once again displaced.

Am I saying all love wears a mask?
That buried motivations spur us on?
That our affection goes out to a ghost
and making do with substitution
restores the lost original? I never
sat beside my dying father's bed,
so maybe I'm condemned to search forever
for old, bedridden, or just any men
with whom to carry on the conversation
peculiar to farewells. My father teased
my mother for her flirting with old men
(other than him, that is). But she had lost
her father at age two. Love's all displaced.

Stuffed animals and guitar magazines
layer the bottom bunk where sprawls a boy.
I part the rubble, pull a chair up, read.
And what is he to me?
This dyad has a nametag: Mother/Son—
label so clear and simple it will soon
fade to a spurious transparency,
as if the natural were here alone,
as if all other ties were second best.
So that when he turns his back upon
this cluttered kingdom (amplifier, lion,
Magic Cards), it will be on a quest
in search of what if not this love displaced?

The End of Summer

Growth marks penciled on the wall
use space to chart the flight of time.
When did he get to be so tall?
I wonder, heading for his room.
Tomorrow he'll be coming home
from camp. How smoothly *home* is said,
as if things ever stayed the same.
Where is the boy I put to bed?

In here for years a nightly pool
of lamplight (but the room was dim)
illuminated a fairy tale
or C.S. Lewis or L. Frank Baum
or a favorite Old Possum poem.
Later he gave me things to read—
Neil Gaiman's gorgeous graphic *Dream*.
Where is the boy I put to bed?

His gaze is hard to gauge, and cool.
Transformation is the theme.
He has long outgrown the small
manageable idea of him
cozily lodged, it used to seem,
in my heart. I look ahead:
steeper slopes already loom.
Where is the boy I put to bed?

Baby pictures fade and peel.
Infancy? Toddlerhood? A dream.
Skip a few years and parents pall.
What can we offer him but some
more of the same? We have become

exactly what he doesn't need,
now that freedom looks sublime.
Where is the boy I put to bed?

Gone, but not quite beyond recall.
Resemblances abruptly come
out of nowhere. From the hill
over which I so clearly am,
I can steal glances back at him.
Something's obscured, but far from dead.
Call it a visionary gleam.
Where is the boy I put to bed?

Jonathan, should this rigid rhyme
scheme leave you cramped, dissatisfied,
make up another—you have time.
Where is the boy I put to bed?

The Crust House

My appetite for talk and yours for sleep
have sometimes led to screaming arguments
in the small hours. The times I want to read
and you to talk, though, fewer sparks fly. Why?
My first thought is self-satisfaction
at being less irascible than you,
gentler in my denials; then I see
it's also true you take more equably
than I to being told to wait till later.
Nights I want to spoon you and you thirst
only for unobstructed plains of sleep,
dark, cool, unnudged, unrumpled—are these balanced
by nights you move to embrace me
and I wriggle irritably away,
burrow toward oblivion, even kick?
Both of us have said and have enacted
No so many times
a hefty edifice of disappointment
is easy to envision, like the crust house
someone's German governess described
as being constructed of discarded toast crusts
willful children leave on the edge of their plates.
Deep in a dark forest,
Itchy, drafty, sinister, this cabin
built not of logs but crusts as hard as rock
(the children, exiled there, must live in it
or eat it up or both)—
is that where we live?

Marriage, I wrote ten years ago,
is a cathedral of the unfinished,
not always crusty, often rickety,
irritation balanced by frustration,

my gargoyle sticking out its tongue at yours.
Symmetry is needed
to keep the structure standing, more or less.
All those Nos build up within a Yes.
I'm still appalled, amused,
surprised by how predictably you wield
the chill blue blade of Occam's Razor.
Nor does my aging little-sister whine
Play with me! get prettier over time.
But after twenty years of knit connections,
our tuggings at the mutual mesh remind us
(retreating to the corners of the bed
like parentheses, but back to back)
just how tough is the reticulation
of binding ties. We have more information
accumulated than we'll ever need,
more on the shelf than we will ever read.

The Web

Certain words and patterns are like art:
we never know we need them till they happen.
Then there they are, lodged in permanence,
indelible, a family joke, a gesture,
entire system spun out of the void
and woven to knots, to tapestries, to blankets.
Would I slash through it?
This web of love entwined with irritation,
afghan to nap beneath, rat-king of tangles,
hammock to swing in through the years of summer,
nostalgia's shroud: from such tough stuff as this
I'd have to undertake my cruel escape.

The Seamy Side

"I and my women can unsnarl the State,"
Lysistrata told the incredulous Magistrate—
the balled-up politics, the tangled war.
What else was expertise in spinning for?

I've forgotten, if I ever knew,
how to spin or weave or knit or sew.
Nevertheless (we're strolling by the brook
in our summer spate of family talk)

I'm struck by how our stories trace the seams
of childhood trauma, disappointed dreams.
The years are fabric barely held together
with gaping stitches: daughter, sister, mother,

an absent father and an angry son . . .
One marriage, then another comes undone.
That we two scrutinize the underside
whose knots and gaps official versions hide—

the underside, the seamy side, the wrong—
must mean there's been a right side all along,
whose pristine surface in each generation's
maintained without apparent complications,

and ties of kinship are as smooth as silk,
and happy families are all alike.
Not even fiction offers such perfection.
And you and I are far removed from fiction,

quizzical siblings and nostalgic mothers
testing the bonds between our lives and others,
acknowledging the bumpiness beneath—
anger, divorce, abandonment, and death.

Let's face it: it's a story after all,
this tangled yarn of families, this ball
we sociably rewind as narrative
that instead of reading we must live.

But now our walk and talk provide a breather,
a little loophole, happy ever after.
Surviving on the seamy side, we tell
each other versions of an endless tale.